Childhood is a wonderful time in one's life. However, when a parent or loved one is stricken with a critical illness, it can become a very frightening time for a child. The child's world is often turned upside down, and feelings of security become threatened.

I have always used books to help explain things to my children. Books are excellent vehicles that help us **start discussions** concerning some very important and difficult issues. Children need to understand what is happening to a sick parent or loved one and how their lives are going to be affected. The unknown can be frightening for anyone at any age, but with the imagination of a child, the unknown can become a terrifying experience.

Childhood is a time of wonder, joy and discovery; a time one needs truth, love and security.

By sharing some of our family experiences with you in this book, I hope I will be able to stimulate conversations between you and any young child who needs to understand what is happening in his or her world.

At the end of the story I have provided a list of suggestions that I hope you find useful when trying to help a young child during this difficult time. Some of these suggestions are part of this story and are easily identified, as they appear in a different type style.

My best wishes to you,

Carolyn

For Kurt William,
Caprice-Ann,
and Eric Lee,
with all my love.

Text copyright ©1994 by Carolyn Stearns Parkinson
Illustrations copyright ©1994 by Elaine Verstraete
"M&M" and "M" are registered trademarks of Mars, Inc.
All rights reserved. No part of this book may be reproduced
or transmitted in any form or by any means, electronic or
mechanical, including photocopying, recording or by
any information storage or retrieval system, without permission
in writing from the publisher.
Printed in the U.S.A.

First printing April 1996
Library of Congress Catalog Card Number 93-086178
ISBN 0-9630287-1-5
SAN 297-4940

Solace Publishing, Inc.
P.O. Box 567
Folsom, CA 95763-0567
1-800-984-9015

Mommy's In The Hospital Again

By Carolyn Stearns Parkinson
Illustrated by Elaine Verstraete

SOLACE PUBLISHING, INC.

E ric eagerly counts, "One, two, three, four, five... **five** more days!"

"Daddy," Eric calls as he hurries downstairs, "Daddy! Only **five** more days until my birthday!"

Eric looks at his Daddy and asks, "Daddy, do you think Mommy will really be home from the hospital for my birthday?"

"I think so," says Daddy. "The doctor said she could come home today or tomorrow. Mommy is going to call this morning to let us know when."

Eric knows that Mommy and Daddy always tell him the truth. It makes him feel better to understand what is happening to his Mommy.

"Daddy?" asks Eric very seriously. "Is Mommy all better now?"

"She is not all better, Eric. The doctors do not know if they can *make* her all better, but they are helping her to *feel* better. Why don't you make Mommy one of your special pictures while I get ready to go to work?"

The phone rings just as Daddy heads upstairs to get dressed for work.

"Eric," says Daddy, "that was Mommy. She can come home tomorrow. We'll go see Mommy tonight after dinner."

Eric works hard to finish the picture of his big brother, Kurt, and his sister, Caprice-Ann, playing ball with him in their backyard.

The day goes by slowly for Eric. Grandma tries to keep him busy playing games, but he just isn't interested. Finally, Daddy is home from work and they have dinner. It seems to take a long time before they are ready to go see Mommy. Eric wants to talk with her about his **Special Day.**

"Mommy," asks Eric, "are you coming home tomorrow?"

"Yes, Eric," Mommy replies.

"Good, I don't want you to miss my birthday and my first day of school."

"No, Eric, I'm not going to miss your **Special Day**. I should be home by lunch time tomorrow."

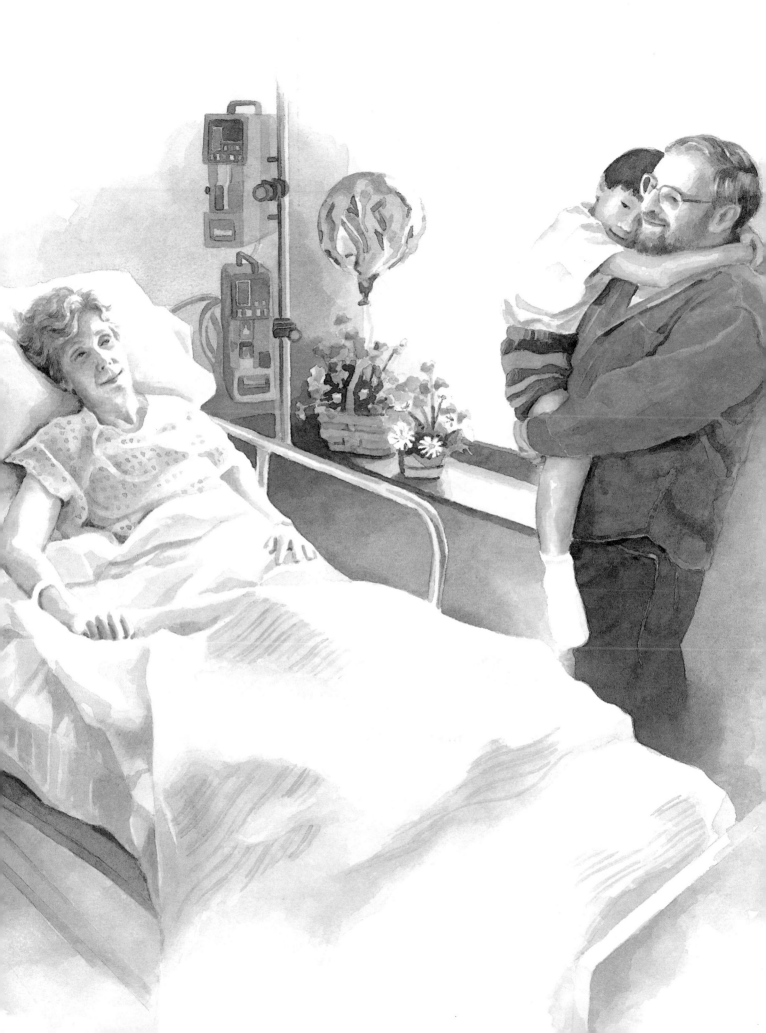

Mommy puts her hand on Eric's hand. "Eric, you do know that if, for some reason, Mommy could not come home in time for your birthday and your first day of school, *almost* everything would still happen. You would still have your party. You would still get your presents, and you would still take cookies to school for your birthday."

"But Mommy, I would miss you."

"I know honey, but you really would have a nice birthday even if Mommy could not be there."

Eric thinks about what Mommy said as he puts his picture on the wall across from her bed. He knows that it makes Mommy happy that Kurt is busy with the show choir at school and that Caprice-Ann is working hard for an ice skating competition. Mommy is glad that he still goes to his swimming lessons. She doesn't like a lot of changes just because she is sick.

"Now," Mommy says with a smile, "it is time for you to go home. I will see you tomorrow."

The next morning, Daddy and Eric drive to the hospital to get Mommy. She is happy to go home, but she is tired.

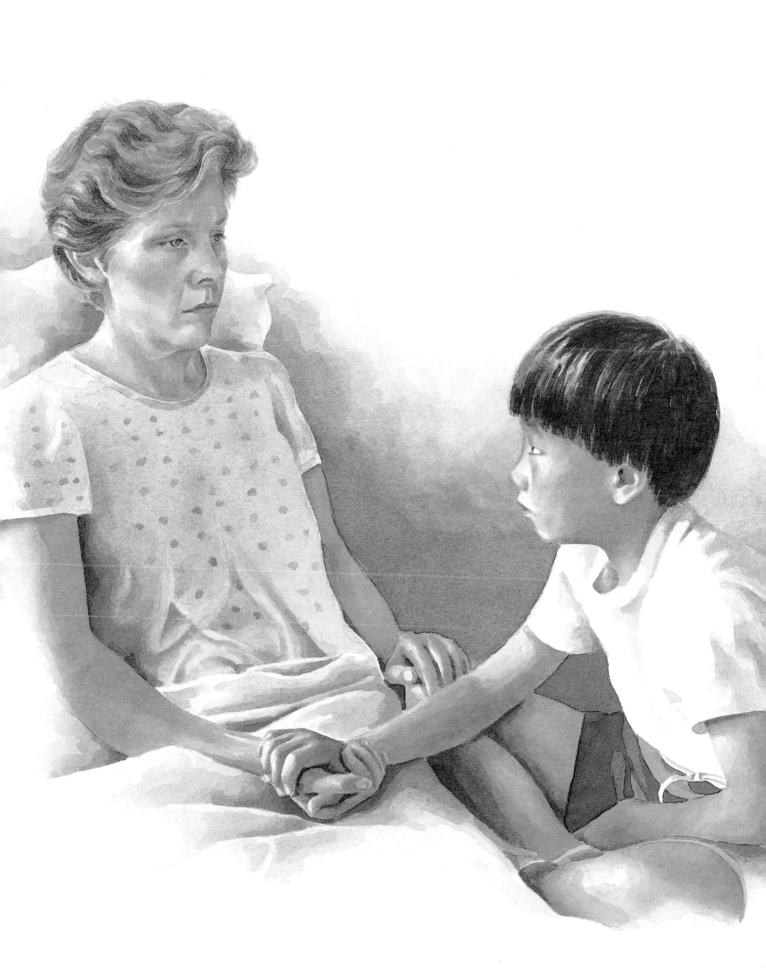

The next two days are busy. Eric and Mommy talk about his Special Day and what they need to do.

They decide that they will make Eric's favorite M&M™ cookies for him to take to school for his birthday.

Mommy asks Eric if he could have only **one** present for his birthday, what would he want. It did not take Eric long to tell her he would like a real camera.

Eric likes helping his Mommy, and they have a lot of fun filling the party bags.

Eric wakes up early the next morning. He hurries into Mommy's room, but her bed is empty. He looks everywhere, but he can't find her or Daddy. Eric becomes very upset.

Kurt hears Eric and quickly finds him. They go into Caprice-Ann's room and wake her up.

Kurt tells them that Mommy is very sick again and had to go back to the hospital during the night. He says that Daddy called and told him that Mommy had to have another operation right away. Daddy will call when it is over.

As Kurt, Caprice-Ann and Eric wait for Dad to call, they feel very angry and scared. Why did this have to happen to their Mom again? What will happen to them?

Finally the phone rings! Kurt anxiously picks up the phone and talks with Dad.

When he puts the phone down, Caprice-Ann asks, "How is Mom?"

"Can we go see her?" asks Eric.

"Mom is going to be all right," replies Kurt, "and we can go to the hospital this afternoon."

"I want to go now!" demands Eric.

"Eric, Mommy is sound asleep because of the operation. She may be awake later this afternoon. So, we will leave around three o'clock," says Kurt.

Kurt, Caprice-Ann and Eric feel better knowing the operation is over and Mom is doing better. They are anxious to see her and, Eric keeps close watch on the clock until it is time to leave.

At the hospital, Kurt, Caprice-Ann and Eric sit with Dad in Mom's room. Mom is sound asleep.

"Daddy? Is Mommy really going to be all right?" asks Eric.

"Yes, Eric, she should be all right, but it is going to take time for Mommy to get strong again," Daddy answers.

"Has she been sleeping all day?" asks Caprice-Ann.

"Yes, honey. The nurses give her medicine for the pain and that also helps her sleep."

Eric looks at all the medicine his Mommy is getting. Daddy has told him what the medicine is and how it will help her.

After awhile Eric becomes restless. It is hard to be quiet for a long time.

"Dad, I think we should go now," Kurt says.

"I don't want to," Eric weeps.

Daddy gives Eric a big hug and says, "You can come again tomorrow, Eric. Maybe Mommy will be awake then, so you can talk to her."

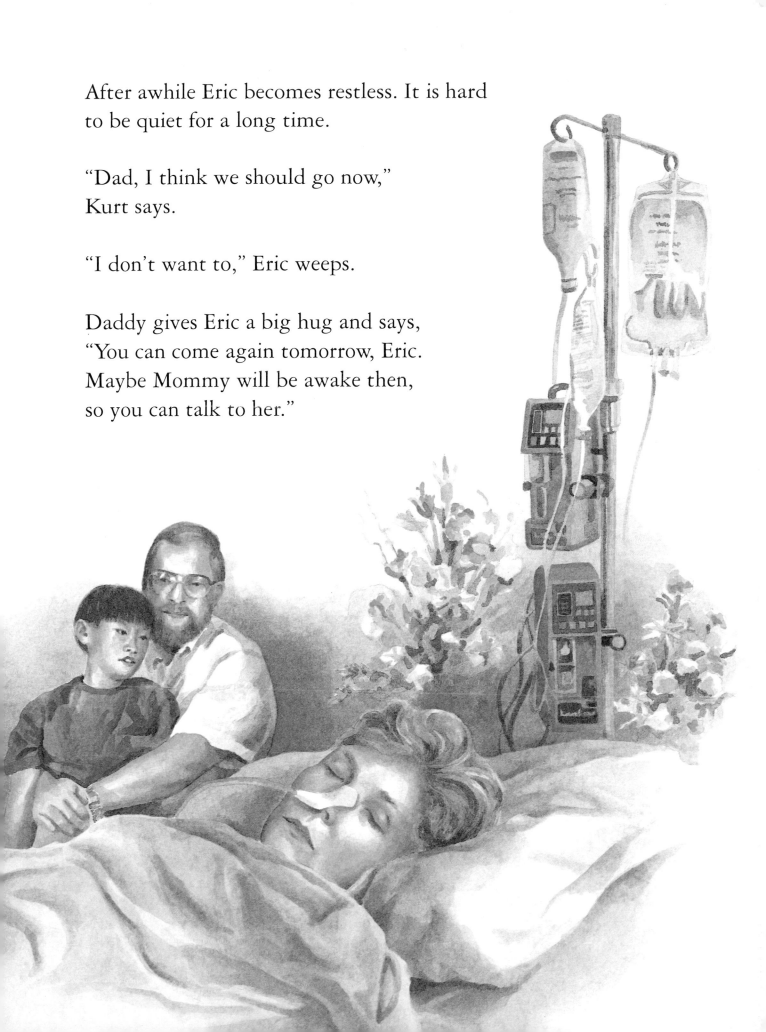

It is a quiet ride home. Eric, Kurt and Caprice-Ann are thinking about the things their parents often talk about with them.

Mommy and Daddy feel it is important for them to continue with their activities and that they do not have to go to the hospital every day. But sometimes it is really hard to deal with their feelings. They are glad that their parents found a support group for them. It helps to talk with other kids who have a parent who is sick - somehow they don't feel quite so alone or different.

Still, they struggle with their own thoughts.

When they arrive home, Kurt and Caprice-Ann help Eric get ready for bed. It has been a long day for Eric, and he begins to think about his maybe **Not**-So-Special Day.

"Eric," says Kurt as he rubs Eric's back, "Mommy is going to be all right. Really! She'll be home soon."

Eric has a hard time settling down as he tells Kurt and Caprice-Ann that he knows that Mommy will not be home for his Special Day. This makes him feel very sad.

"Eric, you will still have your birthday party and maybe we can have one at the hospital, too!" Caprice-Ann says.

Eric likes the idea of a party at the hospital with his Mommy.

"Now," says Kurt, "I'll read you a story so you can go to sleep."

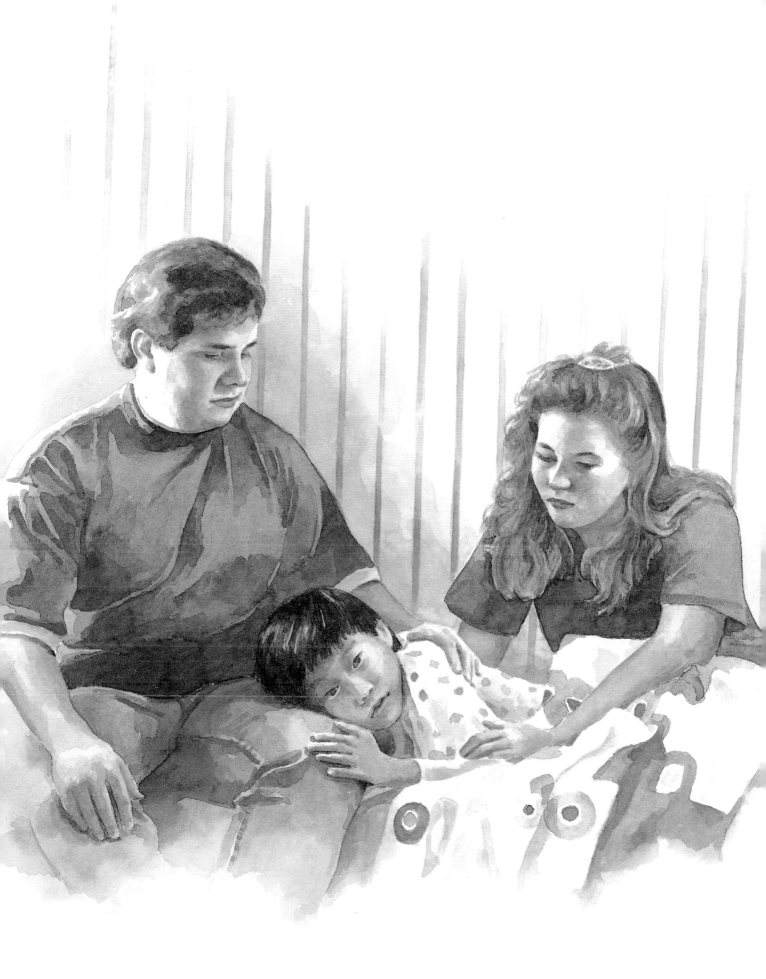

Eric's **Special Day** is here at last! He is 6 years old and is going to start kindergarten.

"We will go to the hospital after your birthday party, Eric. Mommy will want you to tell her all about it, and your first day of school," says Daddy.

"Can I take Mommy a piece of my birthday cake?"

"She would like that," says Daddy.

"Daddy, do you think Mommy will have any presents for me at the hospital?"

"I don't know, Eric. I guess we'll have to wait and see," Daddy says, with just a little *twinkle* in his eye.

"Now, it's time to get ready for school."

Eric's first day of kindergarten is wonderful. Everyone sings "Happy Birthday" to him before they have his M&M™ cookies. He tells his teacher that his Mommy's in the hospital again, so Daddy helped to make his cookies.

Eric knows that Daddy called and talked with his teacher before school started. Daddy feels it is important that his teacher understands about his Mommy and how things are a little different at home.

Soon it is time to go home and get ready for his party.

Eric's birthday party is terrific. He likes all of his presents. His favorite is the big dinosaur from his cousin Erin. All too soon it is time to say goodbye to his friends.

Now, he wants to go to the hospital to tell his Mommy about everything!

"Happy Birthday, Eric. How was your birthday party?" asks Mommy.

"It was so much fun. I got lots of presents, and my cake was really good. I brought you a piece."

"I'm glad you had fun. Thank you for the cake," says Mommy. "How was your first day at school?"

Eric tells Mommy all about his day. He shows her the picture he made for her in school. She likes it, and asks Eric to put it on her wall next to the other picture.

Mommy smiles as she says, "Eric, the nurse told me there was something in my closet all wrapped, and it's for someone whose name starts with an **E**. Maybe you should take a look."

Eric walks over to the closet and finds a bright blue package with a white bow and the letter **E** on it.

He quickly opens his present.

"Mommy! A camera!" shouts Eric. "It's just what I wanted. I want to take some pictures."

Daddy helps Eric put the film in his new camera.

"Smile, Mommy," Eric says, as he takes his first picture.

Eric grins when he sees Caprice-Ann walk into the room with a birthday cake.

Mommy starts to sing "Happy Birthday" to Eric.

Everyone joins in, even the nurse who has come in to check on his Mommy.

"Happy Birthday to you.
Happy Birthday to you.
Happy Birthday, Dear Eric.
Happy Birthday to you."

"Eric," says Mommy, "I love you."

"I love you, too," says Eric. "This really has been

My Special Day."

Support Organizations

American Cancer Society, Inc.
1599 Clifton Road, NE
Atlanta, GA 30329-4251
1-800-ACS-2345

American Diabetes Association
1-800-ADA-DISC

American Heart Association
1-800-242-8721

American Lung Association
1-800-LUNG-USA

American Self-Help Clearinghouse
N.W. Covenant Medical Center
25 Pocono Road
Denville, NJ 07834-2995
201-625-9565
(information on 700+ support groups)

Crohn's & Colitis Foundation
of America, Inc.
386 Park Avenue South, 17th Floor
New York, NY 10016-8804
1-800-343-3637

Kids Adjusting Through Support
600 East Avenue
Rochester, NY 14607
716-232-5287

Kids Helping Kids
Cancer Support and Education Center
Self-Empowerment Programs for
People with Illness
1035 Pine Street
Menlo Park, CA 94025
415-327-6166
415-327-6174 Fax

Muscular Dystrophy Association
602-529-2000

National AIDS Hot Line
1-800-342-AIDS
1-800-344-7432 Spanish (SIDA)
1-800-243-7889 PTY
Hearing Impaired

National Association for Sickle
Cell Disease
200 Corporate Pointe, Suite 495
Culver City, CA 90230-7633
1-800-421-8453
310-216-6363 in CA

National Brain Tumor Foundation
785 Market Street, Suite 1600
San Francisco, CA 94103
1-800-934-CURE
415-284-0209 Fax

National Family Caregivers Association
9621 East Bexhill Drive
Kensington, MD 20895-3104
1-800-896-3650
301-942-6430

National Hospice Organization
1901 N. Moore Street, Suite 901
Arlington, VA 22209
1-800-658-8898

National Mental Health Association
1-800-969-6642

National Multiple Sclerosis Society
1-800-FIGHT MS

The LUPUS Foundation of
America, INC.
1-800-558-0121

Transplant Recipients International
Organization
244 North Bellefield Avenue
Pittsburgh, PA 15213
412-734-5698

Well Spouse Foundation
610 Lexington Ave., Suite 814
New York, NY 10022-6005
1-800-838-0879
212-644-1241

Y-ME Breast Cancer Organization
212 West Van Buren
Chicago, IL 60607
1-800-221-2141
708-799-8228 in IL

Suggestions to help a child when a parent or loved one has a serious and/or prolonged illness.

1. Be open and honest with the child. Explain what is happening in terms that the child can understand.

2. Listen to the child with your ears and eyes. Often the child's body language or behavior will tell you when he or she needs special attention.

3. Love the child. Let the child know it is all right to feel anger and fear, and that he or she is not alone. Explain other peoples reactions that the child may observe (crying, anger, sadness...).

4. Try to keep the child's life as "normal" as possible. A schedule or routine provides a certain amount of security. Attempt to stay on the child's schedule whenever possible.

5. Make the child feel needed. Let the child help you in any way he or she can.

6. Explain what medication is, how it helps, and what side effects it can cause.

7. If possible, introduce the child to the doctors and nurses who are taking care of the parent or loved one.

8. Talk about how hospitals help people. Be sure to explain any special equipment that the child may see when visiting.

9. Contact the child's teachers and let them know what is happening. It is important that people who work with children know when a child is dealing with a stressful situation.

10. Look and seek help for all involved. It can be very difficult to explain an illness and how it affects a child. Look for help from family members, friends, clergy, professional counselors, support groups and books.

The Author

When Carolyn Stearns Parkinson, a professional educator and mother of three children, was diagnosed with cancer in 1987, she tried to find a simple straightforward book that would help her young children understand and cope with the challenges of the disease. Unfortunately she couldn't find what she was looking for. So she decided to write *My Mommy Has Cancer*. This moving story - based entirely on the Parkinson family's experiences - was published in 1991. Since then, it has helped more than 100,000 families deal with the impact of the serious illness of a parent or loved one. *Mommy's In The Hospital Again* is Carolyn's second published work.

When she is not occupied with the demands of writing, publishing, and raising three wonderful children, Carolyn speaks about her books and the stresses that a serious illness can place on a family. She also enjoys reading, walking, traveling, and most of all, her family and friends.

The Illustrator

Elaine Verstraete is rapidly earning a national reputation for her sensitive watercolor illustrations of families and children. A 1984 graduate of Syracuse University with a Bachelor of Fine Arts degree, Elaine has worked for a wide variety of clients, including national health organizations, children's book publishers, magazines and leading corporations. An active skier, cyclist and canoe paddler, she currently lives in a house that she helped build by hand in the scenic Bristol hills of upstate New York.

Carolyn would like to give a very special **Thank You** to Eric's 5th grade class for their help in picking the cover for this book.